A GRATITUDE JOURNAL
FOR KIDS BY

HELPING CREATE
A HAPPIER YOU

A GRATITUDE JOURNAL FOR KIDS BY AWESOME INC™
HELPING CREATE A HAPPIER YOU
WWW.AWESOMEENDSIN.ME

Copyright © AwesoME Inc™.
Text by Rebekah Lipp & Nicole Perry.
Cover design, illustration and typeset by Nicole Perry
(except where stated).

All rights reserved. Except for the purpose of fair review. this book or any portion thereof may not be reproduced or used in any manner whatsoever without the express written permission of the publisher. No reproduction may be made, whether by photocopying or by any other means, unless a licence has been obtained from the publisher or its agent.

1st edition published in 2016.
This edition published in 2018.

Published by ME Incorporated Limited
PO Box 95158, Swanson, Auckland 0653, New Zealand

IT IS THE SIMPLE THINGS IN LIFE THAT CAN REALLY MAKE YOU FEEL HAPPY, IF YOU STOP AND NOTICE.

Sometimes life can get you down, so this book is all about helping you think of the things that are truly great about being alive.

Practising gratitude each day makes you feel good, makes you smarter, healthier and over time can really help on those days that aren't so great (we all have those from time to time). Go to the back of the book to find some more awesome facts about how practising gratitude helps you.

Look at our example (page 7), you can see a GRATITUDE section where each day you fill in at least three new things that you are grateful for. There are literally hundreds of things that we can be thankful for like hanging out with your friends, doctors to help if we are sick, a roof over our heads, our family, our body and all of the amazing things it can do, food to eat, a sunny day, feeling loved by someone .... so many things if you stop and notice. Use our prompts on page 6 if you get stuck.

You will also see a HAPPINESS SCALE on the edge of each page. Colour this in and it will give you a great idea of how happy you have been when you flick back through the pages. If you aren't so happy most of the time, maybe you need to talk to someone about what could be making you feel so low. So, each day make sure to colour in your happiness scale based on how you feel that day.

We have also included a BLANK FACE for you to fill in what mood you are in today. Are you happy, content or excited? Or are you feeling sad, angry or anxious? Don't be afraid to express your feelings, sometimes it can help you to understand them.

Scattered throughout the pages of this book you will find some fun activities too... Fill in a little about yourself, what makes you happy, things you love, and awesome things that happen to you. Sometimes it will be the little things that were great like a hug someone gave you when you felt upset, or playing computer games. Get creative and use lots of colour.

There are also pages with SELF-CARE and HAPPINESS TIPS and COLOURING IN pages drawn by kids like you! Did you know that concentrating on something like colouring can help if you are feeling anxious or stressed. So, if you are feeling overwhelmed or angry, sad or bored, open up this journal and create a masterpiece.

This journal is all about changing the way we look at things AND the way we think about things. The world we live in can be a little crazy at times, there is a lot of pressure to have the right clothing, computer games and other stuff. There is pressure to look a certain way and to be the best at something. It can all get overwhelming, but with gratitude as part of your life you will soon realise that all that stuff isn't what makes you happy. Happiness can't be bought at a store, it is the simple things in life, like walking on the beach and laughing with friends.

NOTHING COMPLICATED, JUST SIMPLE STUFF.

We challenge you to try and complete this book and we would love for you to tell us (or your parents) how it makes you feel at the end when you can read back all that positive stuff you have written about.

Remember AWESOME ENDS IN ME – you are unique, irreplaceable and awesome!

We hope you love this journal.
With the hugest gratitude,

AWESOME INC. – HELPING CREATE A HAPPIER YOU
WWW.AWESOMEENDSIN.ME

I AM GRATEFUL FOR:

- THE WORLD
- NATURE & SPORT
- EXERCISE & SPORT
- MOTHER EARTH
- SOMEONE SHOWING YOU GRATITUDE
- DOING SOMETHING ON GRASS
- WALKING BAREFOOT FOR THE FIRST TIME
- FAVOURITE TV SHOW
- THE MOON AND STARS
- BEING INVITED SOMEWHERE
- WINNING A GAME
- QUIET MOMENTS
- DOCTORS / NURSES
- ROADS & TRANSPORT
- BLANKETS TO KEEP YOU WARM
- YOUR FRIENDS
- SNOW
- HELPING OTHERS
- CHOCOLATE
- BOOKS & READING
- TREES / FLOWERS
- YOUR OWN BED
- FEELING HAPPY
- BEING ON TIME
- YOUR BODY & LEGS & ARMS & EYES
- LOVE THAT ANOTHER PERSON SHOWS YOU
- GOING TO SCHOOL / HOME SCHOOL
- RUNNING WATER / HOT SHOWERS
- SHOPS
- TAKEAWAYS / ORDERING IN
- A GOOD MOVIE
- ANIMALS & PETS
- LAUGHTER
- THE SUN IS SHINING
- GOING ON HOLIDAY
- KINDNESS FROM OTHERS
- A WALK/SWIM AT THE BEACH
- YOUR FAMILY
- YOUR HEALTH
- CLOTHING & SHOES
- THE WEEKEND
- SLEEPING IN
- A FAVOURITE MEAL
- RAIN
- YOUR PARENTS
- DANCING
- MUSIC & SINGING

IF YOU GET STUCK USE THESE EXAMPLES FOR INSPIRATION

6 December 2016
DATE

TODAY I AM... →

HAPPY

TODAY I AM GRATEFUL FOR...

1. The sun is shining and it makes me feel HAPPY!

2. I scored a goal at football and my team won 2-1

3. My legs because they help me run fast.

THANK YOU, THANK YOU, THANK YOU
FOR ALL THE AMAZING THINGS IN MY LIFE!

MY HAPPINESS SCALE

25 WAYS TO » YOU «

SIT IN NATURE

TURN OFF ALL ELECTRONICS

DANCE LIKE NO-ONE IS WATCHING

TAKE A SHOWER OR BATH

MAKE YOUR BED

WALK BAREFOOT ON THE GRASS

HAVE A HEALTHY SNACK

TALK TO A FRIEND

HUG A PET

WRITE IN THIS JOURNA

DO SOMETHING NEW

READ A BOOK

GO FOR A RUN

CLIMB A TREE

SIT IN THE SUN

DO SOME COLOURING IN

LAY ON YOUR BACK AND WATCH THE CLOUDS

GO FOR A WALK

LISTEN TO MUSIC

TAKE SOME DEEP BELLY BREATHS

VISUALISE SOMETHING AWESOME

CHANGE YOUR ENVIRONMENT

DO SOME MEDITATION

WATCH SOMETHING FUNNY

DO SOMETHING NICE FOR SOMEON

WHEN YOU ARE FEELING DOWN, USE THESE IDEAS FOR SOME SELF-CARE.

TODAY I AM...

DATE

TODAY I AM GRATEFUL FOR...

1. MY MOM
   MY DAD
2. MY SISTR
3.

THANK YOU, THANK YOU, THANK YOU
FOR ALL THE AMAZING THINGS IN MY LIFE!

DATE: NOveNSose

TODAY I AM... →

TODAY I AM GRATEFUL FOR...

1. MY BEYBLADES

2. Quinn

3. BEYBLADE Show

MY HAPPINESS SCALE

THANK YOU, THANK YOU, THANK YOU
FOR ALL THE AMAZING THINGS IN MY LIFE!

Jun 1/2023

TODAY I AM... →

TODAY I AM GRATEFUL FOR...

1. My kids. Ariya & Arsen

2. Arsen's smile smell

3. Arsen's kisses
   I ♡
   U

THANK YOU, THANK YOU, THANK YOU
FOR ALL THE AMAZING THINGS IN MY LIFE!

MY HAPPINESS SCALE

TODAY I AM... ←

DATE

TODAY I AM GRATEFUL FOR...

1.

2.

3.

MY HAPPINESS SCALE

THANK YOU, THANK YOU, THANK YOU
FOR ALL THE AMAZING THINGS IN MY LIFE!

14 #CREATEHAPPINESS

DATE

TODAY I AM... →

TODAY I AM GRATEFUL FOR...

1.

2.

3.

THANK YOU, THANK YOU, THANK YOU
FOR ALL THE AMAZING THINGS IN MY LIFE!

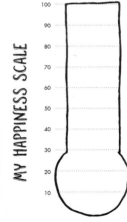

MY HAPPINESS SCALE

WWW.AWESOMEENDSIN.ME

TODAY
I AM...
←

DATE

TODAY I AM GRATEFUL FOR...

1.

2.

3.

MY HAPPINESS SCALE

100
90
80
70
60
50
40
30
20
10

THANK YOU, THANK YOU, THANK YOU
FOR ALL THE AMAZING THINGS IN MY LIFE!

16 #CREATEHAPPINESS

DATE

TODAY I AM...

TODAY I AM GRATEFUL FOR...

1.

2.

3.

THANK YOU, THANK YOU, THANK YOU
FOR ALL THE AMAZING THINGS IN MY LIFE!

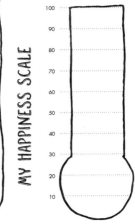

WWW.AWESOMEENDSIN.ME 17

TODAY I AM...

DATE

TODAY I AM GRATEFUL FOR...

1.

2.

3.

THANK YOU, THANK YOU, THANK YOU
FOR ALL THE AMAZING THINGS IN MY LIFE!

DATE

TODAY I AM... →

TODAY I AM GRATEFUL FOR...

1.

2.

3.

THANK YOU, THANK YOU, THANK YOU
FOR ALL THE AMAZING THINGS IN MY LIFE!

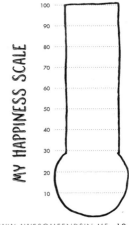

MY HAPPINESS SCALE

WWW.AWESOMEENDSIN.ME

LAUGHTER is the BEST MEDICINE

HAPPINESS TIP:

Laugh as much as you can, whenever you can, and learn to laugh at yourself too … it is the best medicine. Even if you force yourself to laugh, by faking it, for long enough, at some point you will genuinely start laughing.

Laughter can strengthen your immune system, help boost your energy and diminish pain, and also protect you from the effects of stress.

WHAT MAKES ME LAUGH...

USE WORDS AND PICTURES TO DESCRIBE WHAT MAKES YOU LAUGH

DATE

TODAY I AM... →

TODAY I AM GRATEFUL FOR...

1.

2.

3.

THANK YOU, THANK YOU, THANK YOU
FOR ALL THE AMAZING THINGS IN MY LIFE!

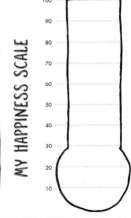

MY HAPPINESS SCALE

100
90
80
70
60
50
40
30
20
10

WWW.AWESOMEENDSIN.ME

DATE

TODAY I AM... →

TODAY I AM GRATEFUL FOR...

1.

2.

3.

THANK YOU, THANK YOU, THANK YOU
FOR ALL THE AMAZING THINGS IN MY LIFE!

MY HAPPINESS SCALE

WWW.AWESOMEENDSIN.ME

DATE

TODAY I AM... →

TODAY I AM GRATEFUL FOR...

1.

2.

3.

THANK YOU, THANK YOU, THANK YOU
FOR ALL THE AMAZING THINGS IN MY LIFE!

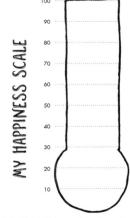

MY HAPPINESS SCALE

WWW.AWESOMEENDSIN.ME

DATE ....

TODAY I AM... →

TODAY I AM GRATEFUL FOR...

1.

2.

3.

THANK YOU, THANK YOU, THANK YOU
FOR ALL THE AMAZING THINGS IN MY LIFE!

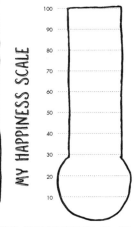

MY HAPPINESS SCALE

100
90
80
70
60
50
40
30
20
10

WWW.AWESOMEENDSIN.ME 29

TODAY I AM...

DATE

TODAY I AM GRATEFUL FOR...

1.

2.

3.

THANK YOU, THANK YOU, THANK YOU
FOR ALL THE AMAZING THINGS IN MY LIFE!

MY HAPPINESS SCALE

DRAWING BY LEO, AGE 9

DATE ....

TODAY I AM... →

TODAY I AM GRATEFUL FOR...

1.

2.

3.

THANK YOU, THANK YOU, THANK YOU
FOR ALL THE AMAZING THINGS IN MY LIFE!

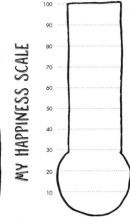

MY HAPPINESS SCALE

WWW.AWESOMEENDSIN.ME 33

TODAY I AM...

DATE

TODAY I AM GRATEFUL FOR...

1.

2.

3.

MY HAPPINESS SCALE

100
90
80
70
60
50
40
30
20
10

THANK YOU, THANK YOU, THANK YOU
FOR ALL THE AMAZING THINGS IN MY LIFE!

34 #CREATEHAPPINESS

DATE

TODAY I AM... →

TODAY I AM GRATEFUL FOR...

1.

2.

3.

THANK YOU, THANK YOU, THANK YOU
FOR ALL THE AMAZING THINGS IN MY LIFE!

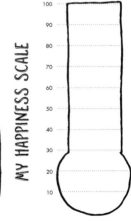

MY HAPPINESS SCALE

WWW.AWESOMEENDSIN.ME

DATE

TODAY I AM... →

TODAY I AM GRATEFUL FOR...

1.

2.

3.

THANK YOU, THANK YOU, THANK YOU
FOR ALL THE AMAZING THINGS IN MY LIFE!

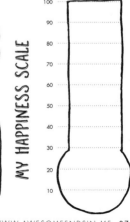

MY HAPPINESS SCALE

TODAY I AM... ←

DATE

TODAY I AM GRATEFUL FOR...

1.

2.

3.

MY HAPPINESS SCALE

THANK YOU, THANK YOU, THANK YOU
FOR ALL THE AMAZING THINGS IN MY LIFE!

DATE

TODAY I AM... →

TODAY I AM GRATEFUL FOR...

1.

2.

3.

THANK YOU, THANK YOU, THANK YOU
FOR ALL THE AMAZING THINGS IN MY LIFE!

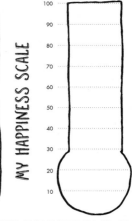

MY HAPPINESS SCALE

WWW.AWESOMEENDSIN.ME

GET OUTSIDE ← and ⫷ MOVE

HAPPINESS TIP:

Going for a walk outside, in the bush or at the beach, makes you feel more refreshed and energetic, and less tense and angry.

Exercise increases endorphines (those feel-good brain chemicals) and reduces the level of stress hormones in your body. The mood benefits of just 20 minutes of exercise can last up to 12 hours.

THINGS I LOVE TO DO
OUTSIDE

USE WORDS AND PICTURES TO DESCRIBE WHAT YOU LOVE TO DO

DATE

TODAY I AM...

TODAY I AM GRATEFUL FOR...

1.

2.

3.

THANK YOU, THANK YOU, THANK YOU
FOR ALL THE AMAZING THINGS IN MY LIFE!

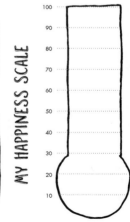

MY HAPPINESS SCALE

WWW.AWESOMEENDSIN.ME

DATE

TODAY I AM... →

TODAY I AM GRATEFUL FOR...

1.

2.

3.

THANK YOU, THANK YOU, THANK YOU
FOR ALL THE AMAZING THINGS IN MY LIFE!

MY HAPPINESS SCALE

DATE

TODAY I AM...

TODAY I AM GRATEFUL FOR...

1.

2.

3.

THANK YOU, THANK YOU, THANK YOU
FOR ALL THE AMAZING THINGS IN MY LIFE!

MY HAPPINESS SCALE

WWW.AWESOMEENDSIN.ME

DATE

TODAY I AM... →

TODAY I AM GRATEFUL FOR...

1.

2.

3.

THANK YOU, THANK YOU, THANK YOU
FOR ALL THE AMAZING THINGS IN MY LIFE!

MY HAPPINESS SCALE

WWW.AWESOMEENDSIN.ME

DRAWING BY ARABELLA, AGE 7

TODAY I AM...

DATE

TODAY I AM GRATEFUL FOR...

1.

2.

3.

MY HAPPINESS SCALE

THANK YOU, THANK YOU, THANK YOU
FOR ALL THE AMAZING THINGS IN MY LIFE!

52 #CREATEHAPPINESS

DATE

TODAY I AM... →

TODAY I AM GRATEFUL FOR...

1.

2.

3.

THANK YOU, THANK YOU, THANK YOU
FOR ALL THE AMAZING THINGS IN MY LIFE!

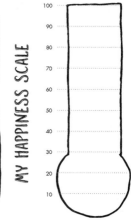

MY HAPPINESS SCALE

WWW.AWESOMEENDSIN.ME

DATE

TODAY I AM... →

TODAY I AM GRATEFUL FOR...

1.

2.

3.

THANK YOU, THANK YOU, THANK YOU
FOR ALL THE AMAZING THINGS IN MY LIFE!

MY HAPPINESS SCALE

DATE

TODAY I AM GRATEFUL FOR...

1.

2.

3.

THANK YOU, THANK YOU, THANK YOU
FOR ALL THE AMAZING THINGS IN MY LIFE!

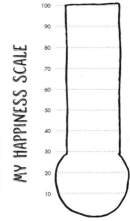

MY HAPPINESS SCALE

WWW.AWESOMEENDSIN.ME

DATE

TODAY I AM...

TODAY I AM GRATEFUL FOR...

1.

2.

3.

THANK YOU, THANK YOU, THANK YOU
FOR ALL THE AMAZING THINGS IN MY LIFE!

MY HAPPINESS SCALE

SOMETHING AWESOME
THAT HAPPENED TO ME

USE WORDS AND PICTURES TO DESCRIBE WHAT HAPPENED

DATE: ....

TODAY I AM... → (··)

TODAY I AM GRATEFUL FOR...

1.

2.

3.

THANK YOU, THANK YOU, THANK YOU
FOR ALL THE AMAZING THINGS IN MY LIFE!

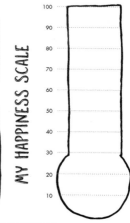

MY HAPPINESS SCALE

WWW.AWESOMEENDSIN.ME

DATE

TODAY I AM... →

TODAY I AM GRATEFUL FOR...

1.

2.

3.

THANK YOU, THANK YOU, THANK YOU
FOR ALL THE AMAZING THINGS IN MY LIFE!

MY HAPPINESS SCALE

WWW.AWESOMEENDSIN.ME

DATE

TODAY I AM... →

TODAY I AM GRATEFUL FOR...

1.

2.

3.

THANK YOU, THANK YOU, THANK YOU
FOR ALL THE AMAZING THINGS IN MY LIFE!

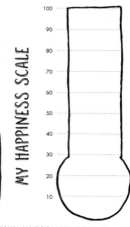

WWW.AWESOMEENDSIN.ME

DATE

TODAY I AM... →

TODAY I AM GRATEFUL FOR...

1.

2.

3.

THANK YOU, THANK YOU, THANK YOU
FOR ALL THE AMAZING THINGS IN MY LIFE!

MY HAPPINESS SCALE

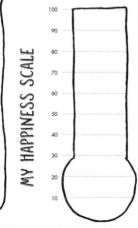

WWW.AWESOMEENDSIN.ME

HAPPINESS IS CONTAGIOUS

HAPPINESS TIP:

We are all connected, so what we feel affects the people around us. Smile at at stranger you pass on the street. If you make eye contact, they will likely smile back. You just made them happy too!

Did you know smiling may increase your lifespan, lower stress hormones and blood pressure. The muscles in your face send messages that alter the area of the brain that affect emotions. Smiling actually stimulates those feel-good areas of the brain more than chocolate and money.

THINGS THAT MAKE ME HAPPY!

USE WORDS AND PICTURES TO DESCRIBE WHAT MAKES YOU HAPPY

DATE ....

TODAY I AM...

TODAY I AM GRATEFUL FOR...

1.

2.

3.

THANK YOU, THANK YOU, THANK YOU
FOR ALL THE AMAZING THINGS IN MY LIFE!

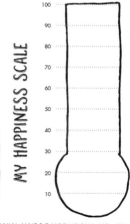

MY HAPPINESS SCALE

WWW.AWESOMEENDSIN.ME

DATE

TODAY I AM...

TODAY I AM GRATEFUL FOR...

1.

2.

3.

THANK YOU, THANK YOU, THANK YOU
FOR ALL THE AMAZING THINGS IN MY LIFE!

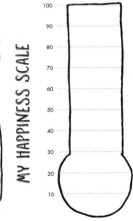

WWW.AWESOMEENDSIN.ME

DATE

TODAY I AM... →

TODAY I AM GRATEFUL FOR...

1.

2.

3.

THANK YOU, THANK YOU, THANK YOU
FOR ALL THE AMAZING THINGS IN MY LIFE!

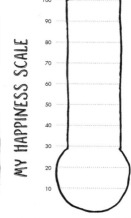

MY HAPPINESS SCALE

WWW.AWESOMEENDSIN.ME

DATE

TODAY I AM... →

TODAY I AM GRATEFUL FOR...

1.

2.

3.

THANK YOU, THANK YOU, THANK YOU
FOR ALL THE AMAZING THINGS IN MY LIFE!

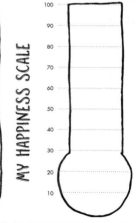

MY HAPPINESS SCALE

WWW.AWESOMEENDSIN.ME

DRAWING BY KELLY, AGE 14

DATE ....

TODAY I AM... →

TODAY I AM GRATEFUL FOR...

1.

2.

3.

THANK YOU, THANK YOU, THANK YOU
FOR ALL THE AMAZING THINGS IN MY LIFE!

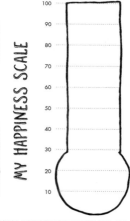

MY HAPPINESS SCALE

WWW.AWESOMEENDSIN.ME

DATE

TODAY I AM...

TODAY I AM GRATEFUL FOR...

1.

2.

3.

THANK YOU, THANK YOU, THANK YOU
FOR ALL THE AMAZING THINGS IN MY LIFE!

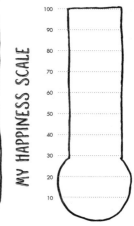

MY HAPPINESS SCALE

WWW.AWESOMEENDSIN.ME

DATE

TODAY I AM... →

TODAY I AM GRATEFUL FOR...

1.

2.

3.

THANK YOU, THANK YOU, THANK YOU
FOR ALL THE AMAZING THINGS IN MY LIFE!

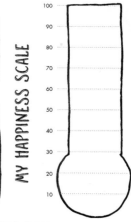

MY HAPPINESS SCALE

DATE

TODAY I AM...

TODAY I AM GRATEFUL FOR...

1.

2.

3.

THANK YOU, THANK YOU, THANK YOU
FOR ALL THE AMAZING THINGS IN MY LIFE!

MY HAPPINESS SCALE

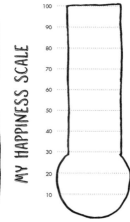

WWW.AWESOMEENDSIN.ME

DO something >> NICE for SOMEONE ELSE

HAPPINESS TIP:

Giving to others releases natural feel-good chemicals in your brain that activate those areas (of the brain) associated with trust, pleasure and social connection. Spending money or doing something for others leads to higher levels of happiness, and increases the chance that you will be generous in the future. This creates a positive feedback loop of generosity and happiness. The trick is to do something without being asked.

THINGS I CAN DO
FOR SOMEONE ELSE

USE WORDS AND PICTURES TO SHOW YOUR IDEAS

DATE

TODAY I AM... →

TODAY I AM GRATEFUL FOR...

1.

2.

3.

THANK YOU, THANK YOU, THANK YOU
FOR ALL THE AMAZING THINGS IN MY LIFE!

MY HAPPINESS SCALE

WWW.AWESOMEENDSIN.ME

DATE

TODAY I AM... →

TODAY I AM GRATEFUL FOR...

1.

2.

3.

THANK YOU, THANK YOU, THANK YOU
FOR ALL THE AMAZING THINGS IN MY LIFE!

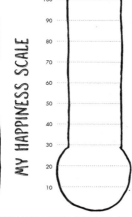

MY HAPPINESS SCALE

DATE ....

TODAY I AM... →

TODAY I AM GRATEFUL FOR...

1.

2.

3.

THANK YOU, THANK YOU, THANK YOU
FOR ALL THE AMAZING THINGS IN MY LIFE!

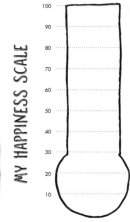

MY HAPPINESS SCALE

DATE

TODAY I AM...

TODAY I AM GRATEFUL FOR...

1.

2.

3.

THANK YOU, THANK YOU, THANK YOU
FOR ALL THE AMAZING THINGS IN MY LIFE!

MY HAPPINESS SCALE

WWW.AWESOMEENDSIN.ME

SAY ☆ THANK ★ YOU

HAPPINESS TIP:

Say 'Thank you' as much as you can to as many people as you can. Thank them for the little things, like letting you in front of them in line, but also for the big stuff too, like your parents for caring for you or a teacher that believes in you.

Not only will it make them feel happy but it will make you feel more positive emotions, relish good experiences, improve your health, plus help you deal with difficult situations and build stronger relationships with others.

DRAWING BY LILY, AGE 9

TODAY I AM...

DATE ....

TODAY I AM GRATEFUL FOR...

1.

2.

3.

THANK YOU, THANK YOU, THANK YOU
FOR ALL THE AMAZING THINGS IN MY LIFE!

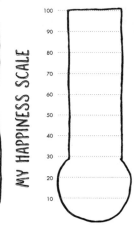

MY HAPPINESS SCALE

WWW.AWESOMEENDSIN.ME 103

DATE

TODAY I AM... →

TODAY I AM GRATEFUL FOR...

1.

2.

3.

THANK YOU, THANK YOU, THANK YOU
FOR ALL THE AMAZING THINGS IN MY LIFE!

MY HAPPINESS SCALE

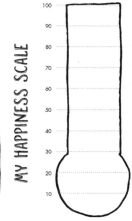

WWW.AWESOMEENDSIN.ME

DATE

TODAY I AM... →

TODAY I AM GRATEFUL FOR...

1.

2.

3.

THANK YOU, THANK YOU, THANK YOU
FOR ALL THE AMAZING THINGS IN MY LIFE!

MY HAPPINESS SCALE

WWW.AWESOMEENDSIN.ME

DATE

TODAY I AM... →

TODAY I AM GRATEFUL FOR...

1.

2.

3.

THANK YOU, THANK YOU, THANK YOU
FOR ALL THE AMAZING THINGS IN MY LIFE!

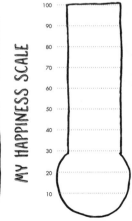

MY HAPPINESS SCALE

WWW.AWESOMEENDSIN.ME 109

Gratitude strengthens the immune system, lowers blood pressure, reduces symptoms of illness, and makes us less bothered by aches and pains. It also encourages us to exercise more and take better care of our health.[1]

GRATITUDE MAKES A PERSON LESS MATERIALISTIC, AND THEREFORE KINDER TO THE ENVIRONMENT.[2]

You can feel more connected to your friends, family, feel better about your school, have higher levels of optimism, increased life satisfaction, and decreased negative feelings.

Kids who practise gratitude show an increase in grateful thinking, appreciation and positive emotions, compared to those who don't practice.[4]

7 WAYS GRATITUDE HELPS YOU

It helps us notice the world around us, and what our blessings are. We start taking less things for granted and feel more awake and alive.[5]

Writing down 3 things you are grateful for can boost happiness better than recalling three times when a person felt a sense of pride in his or her own accomplishments...

After 8 weeks of practicing gratitude a study showed people are able to interact with others better and be more empathetic.[6]

It makes people look for the good in their life more, so it trains their attention to more good things.[7]

1. PROF. ROBERT EMMONS, THE UNIVERSITY OF CALIFORNIA & PROF. MICHAEL MCCULLOUGH, UNIVERSITY OF MIAMI
2. ACCORDING TO A STUDY PRESENTED AT AN AMERICAN PSYCHOLOGICAL ASSOCIATION CONVENTION
3. JEFFREY FROH, ASSOCIATE PROFESSOR, HOFSTRA UNIVERSITY
4. JEFFREY FROH, ASSOCIATE PROFESSOR, HOFSTRA UNIVERSITY
5. DR. KERRY HOWELLS, UNIVERSITY OF TASMANIA
6. DR. EMILIANA SIMON-THOMAS, SCIENCE DIRECTOR, THE GREATER GOOD SCIENCE CENTER, BERKELEY
7. PROF. PHILLIP WATKINS, DEPT OF PSYCHOLOGY, EASTERN WASHINGTON UNIVERSITY

For more facts go to *http://greatergood.berkeley.edu/topic/gratitude*